D0503842

THE
LITTLE BOOK OF
SELF-CARE
· FOR ·
GEMINI

*Simple Ways to Refresh
and Restore—According
to the Stars*

CONSTANCE STELLAS

ADAMS MEDIA

NEW YORK LONDON TORONTO SYDNEY NEW DELHI

Adams Media
An Imprint of Simon & Schuster, Inc.
100 Technology Center Drive
Stoughton, MA 02072

First Adams Media hardcover edition January 2019

ADAMS MEDIA and colophon are trademarks of Simon & Schuster.

For information about special discounts for bulk purchases,
please contact Simon & Schuster Special Sales at 1-866-506-1949 or
business@simonandschuster.com.

The Simon & Schuster Speakers Bureau can bring authors to your live event. For more information or to book an event contact the Simon & Schuster Speakers Bureau at 1-866-248-3049 or visit our website at www.simonspeakers.com.

Interior design by Colleen Cunningham
Interior images © Getty Images; Clipart.com

Manufactured in China

10 9 8 7 6

Library of Congress Cataloging-in-Publication Data has been applied for.

ISBN 978-1-5072-0968-4
ISBN 978-1-5072-0969-1 (ebook)

Dedication

To my witty, multitalented Gemini friends, Bob and Fran,
and my Gemini niece, Rachel, with love and appreciation.

CONTENTS

Acknowledgments

I would like to thank Karen Cooper and everyone at Adams Media who helped with this book. To Brendan O'Neill, Katie Corcoran Lytle, Sarah Doughty, Eileen Mullan, Casey Ebert, Sylvia Davis, and everyone else who worked on the manuscripts. To Frank Rivera, Colleen Cunningham, and Katrina Machado for their work on the book's cover and interior design. I appreciated your team spirit and eagerness to dive into the riches of astrology.

Introduction

It's time for you to have a little *"me" time*—powered by the zodiac. By tapping into your Sun sign's astrological and elemental energies, *The Little Book of Self-Care for Gemini* brings star-powered strength and cosmic relief to your life with self-care guidance tailored specifically for you.

While you may love socializing and being the life of the party, Gemini, this book focuses on your true self. This book provides information on how to incorporate self-care into your life while teaching you just how important astrology is to your overall self-care routine. You'll learn more about yourself as you learn about your sign and its governing element, air. Then you can relax, rejuvenate, and stay balanced with more than one hundred self-care ideas and activities perfect for your Gemini personality.

From trying origami to meditating with crystals, you will find plenty of ways to heal your mind, body, and active spirit. Now, let the stars be your self-care guide!

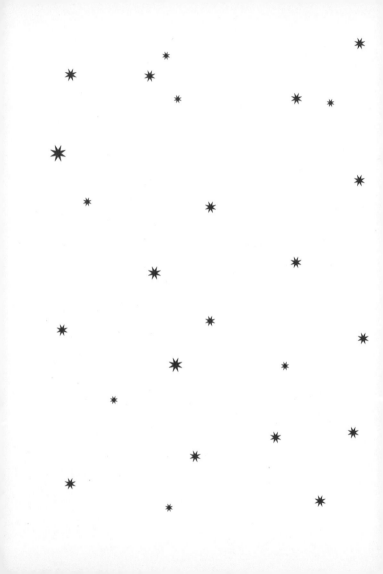

♊

PART 1

SIGNS, ELEMENTS, ── AND ── SELF-CARE

CHAPTER 1

WHAT IS SELF-CARE?

Astrology gives insights into whom to love, when to charge forward into new beginnings, and how to succeed in whatever you put your mind to. When paired with self-care, astrology can also help you relax and reclaim that part of yourself that tends to get lost in the bustle of the day. In this chapter you'll learn what self-care is—for you. (No matter your sign, self-care is more than just lit candles and quiet reflection, though these activities may certainly help you find the renewal that you seek.) You'll also learn how making a priority of personalized self-care activities can benefit you in ways you may not even have thought of. Whether you're a Gemini, a Pisces, or a Taurus, you deserve rejuvenation and renewal that's customized to your sign—this chapter reveals where to begin.

What Self-Care Is

Self-care is any activity that you do to take care of yourself. It rejuvenates your body, refreshes your mind, or realigns your spirit. It relaxes and refuels you. It gets you ready for a new day or a fresh start. It's the practices, rituals, and meaningful activities that you do, just for you, that help you feel safe, grounded, happy, and fulfilled.

The activities that qualify as self-care are amazingly unique and personalized to who you are, what you like, and, in large part, what your astrological sign is. If you're asking questions about what self-care practices are best for those ruled by air and born under the inquisitive eye of Gemini, you'll find answers—and restoration—in Part 2. But, no matter which of those self-care activities speak to you and your unique place in the universe on any given day, it will fall into one of the following self-care categories—each of which pertains to a different aspect of your life:

* Physical self-care
* Emotional self-care
* Social self-care
* Mental self-care
* Spiritual self-care
* Practical self-care

When you practice all of these unique types of self-care—and prioritize your practice to ensure you are choosing the best options for your unique sign and governing element—know that you are actively working to create the version of yourself that the universe intends you to be.

Physical Self-Care

When you practice physical self-care, you make the decision to look after and restore the one physical body that has been bestowed upon you. Care for it. Use it in the best way you can imagine, for that is what the universe wishes you to do. You can't light the world on fire or move mountains if you're not doing everything you can to take care of your physical health.

Emotional Self-Care

Emotional self-care is when you take the time to acknowledge and care for your inner self, your emotional well-being. Whether you're angry or frustrated, happy or joyful, or somewhere in between, emotional self-care happens when you choose to sit with your emotions: when you step away from the noise of daily life that often drowns out or tamps down your authentic self. Emotional self-care lets you see your inner you as the cosmos intend. Once you identify your true emotions, you can either accept them and continue to move forward on your journey or you can try to change any negative emotions for the better. The more you acknowledge your feelings and practice emotional self-care, the more you'll feel the positivity that the universe and your life holds for you.

Social Self-Care

You practice social self-care when you nurture your relationships with others, be they friends, coworkers, or family members. In today's hectic world it's easy to let relationships fall to the wayside, but it's so important to share your life with others—and let others share their lives with you. Social self-care is reciprocal and often karmic. The support and love that you put out into the universe through social self-care is given back to you by those you socialize with—often tenfold.

Mental Self-Care

Mental self-care is anything that keeps your mind working quickly and critically. It helps you cut through the fog of the day, week, or year and ensures that your quick wit and sharp mind are intact and working the way the cosmos intended. Making sure your mind is fit helps you problem-solve, decreases stress since you're not feeling overwhelmed, and keeps you feeling on top of your mental game—no matter your sign or your situation.

Spiritual Self-Care

Spiritual self-care is self-care that allows you to tap into your soul and the soul of the universe and uncover its secrets. Rather than focusing on a particular religion or set of religious beliefs, these types of self-care activities reconnect you with a higher power: the sense that something out there is bigger than you. When you meditate, you connect. When you pray, you connect. Whenever you do something that allows you to experience and marry yourself to the vastness that is the cosmos, you practice spiritual self-care.

Practical Self-Care

Self-care is what you do to take care of yourself, and practical self-care, while not as expansive as the other types, is made up of the seemingly small day-to-day tasks that bring you peace and accomplishment. These practical self-care rituals are important, but are often overlooked. Scheduling a doctor's appointment that you've been putting off is practical self-care. Getting your hair cut is practical self-care. Anything you can check off your list of things to be accomplished gives you a sacred space to breathe and allows the universe more room to bring a beautiful sense of cosmic fulfillment your way.

What Self-Care Isn't

Self-care is restorative. Self-care is clarifying. Self-care is whatever you need to do to make yourself feel secure in the universe.

Now that you know what self-care is, it's also important that you're able to see what self-care isn't. Self-care is not something that you force yourself to do because you think it will be good for you. Some signs are energy in motion and sitting still goes against their place in the universe. Those signs won't feel refreshed by lying in a hammock or sitting down to meditate. Other signs aren't able to ground themselves unless they've found a self-care practice that protects their cosmic need for peace and quiet. Those signs won't find parties, concerts, and loud venues soothing or satisfying. If a certain ritual doesn't bring you peace, clarity, or satisfaction, then it's not right for your sign and you should find something that speaks to you more clearly.

There's a difference though between not finding satisfaction in a ritual that you've tried and not wanting to try a self-care activity because you're tired or stuck in a comfort zone. Sometimes going to the gym or meeting up with friends is the self-care practice that you need to experience—whether engaging in it feels like a downer or not. So consider how you feel when you're actually doing the activity. If it feels invigorating to get on the treadmill or you feel delight when you actually catch up with your friend, the ritual is doing what it should be doing and clearing space for you—among other benefits...

The Benefits of Self-Care

The benefits of self-care are boundless and there's none that's superior to helping you put rituals in place to feel more at home in your body, in your spirit, and in your unique home in the cosmos. There are, however, other benefits to engaging in the practice of self-care that you should know.

Rejuvenates Your Immune System

No matter which rituals are designated for you by the stars, your sign, and its governing element, self-care helps both your body and mind rest, relax, and recuperate. The practice of self-care activates the parasympathetic nervous system (often called the rest and digest system), which slows your heart rate, calms the body, and, overall, helps your body relax and release tension. This act of decompression gives your body the space it needs to build up and strengthen your immune system, which protects you from illness.

Helps You Reconnect—with Yourself

When you practice the ritual of self-care—especially when you customize this practice based on your personal sign and governing element—you learn what you like to do and what you need to do to replenish yourself. Knowing yourself better, and allowing yourself the time and space that you need to focus on your personal needs and desires, gives you the gifts of self-confidence and self-knowledge. Setting time aside to focus on your needs also helps you put busy, must-do things aside, which gives you time to reconnect with yourself and who you are deep inside.

Increases Compassion

Perhaps one of the most important benefits of creating a self-care ritual is that, by focusing on yourself, you become more compassionate to others as well. When you truly take the time to care for yourself and make yourself and your importance in the universe a priority in your own life, you're then able to care for others and see their needs and desires in a new way. You can't pour from an empty dipper, and self-care allows you the space and clarity to do what you can to send compassion out into the world.

Starting a Self-Care Routine

Self-care should be treated as a ritual in your life, something you make the time to pause for, no matter what. You are important. You deserve rejuvenation and a sense of relaxation. You need to open your soul to the gifts that the universe is giving you, and self-care provides you with a way to ensure you're ready to receive those gifts. To begin a self-care routine, start by making yourself the priority. Do the customized rituals in Part 2 with intention, knowing the universe has already given them to you, by virtue of your sign and your governing element.

Now that you understand the role that self-care will hold in your life, let's take a closer look at the connection between self-care and astrology.

CHAPTER 2

SELF-CARE
AND ASTROLOGY

Astrology is the study of the connection between the objects in the heavens (the planets, the stars) and what happens here on earth. Just as the movements of the planets and other heavenly bodies influence the ebb and flow of the tides, so do they influence you—your body, your mind, your spirit. This relationship is ever present and is never more important—or personal—than when viewed through the lens of self-care.

In this chapter you'll learn how the locations of these celestial bodies at the time of your birth affect you and define the self-care activities that will speak directly to you as a Leo, an Aries, a Capricorn, or any of the other zodiac signs. You'll see how the zodiac influences every part of your being and why ignoring its lessons can leave you feeling frustrated and unfulfilled. You'll also realize that, when you perform the rituals of self-care based on your sign, the wisdom of the cosmos will lead you down a path of fulfillment and restoration—to the return of who *you* really are, deep inside.

Zodiac Polarities

In astrology, all signs are mirrored by other signs that are on the opposite side of the zodiac. This polarity ensures that the zodiac is balanced and continues to flow with an unbreakable, even stream of energy. There are two different polarities in the zodiac and each is called by a number of different names:

* Yang/masculine/positive polarity
* Yin/feminine/negative polarity

Each polar opposite embodies a number of opposing traits, qualities, and attributes that will influence which self-care practices will work for or against your sign and your own personal sense of cosmic balance.

Yang

Whether male or female, those who fall under yang, or masculine, signs are extroverted and radiate their energy outward. They are spontaneous, active, bold, and fearless. They move forward in life with the desire to enjoy everything the world has to offer to them, and they work hard to transfer their inspiration and positivity to others so that those individuals may experience the same gifts that the universe offers them. All signs governed by the fire and air elements are yang and hold the potential for these dominant qualities. We will refer to them with masculine pronouns. These signs are:

* Aries
* Leo
* Sagittarius
* Gemini
* Libra
* Aquarius

There are people who hold yang energy who are introverted and retiring. However, by practicing self-care that is customized for your sign and understanding the potential ways to use your energy, you can find a way—perhaps one that's unique to you—to claim your native buoyancy and dominance and engage with the path that the universe opens for you.

Yin

Whether male or female, those who fall under yin, or feminine, signs are introverted and radiate inwardly. They draw people and experiences to them rather than seeking people and experiences in an extroverted way. They move forward in life with an energy that is reflective, receptive, and focused on communication and achieving shared goals. All signs governed by the earth and water elements are yin and hold the potential for these reflective qualities. We will refer to them with feminine pronouns. These signs are:

* Taurus
* Virgo
* Capricorn
* Cancer
* Scorpio
* Pisces

As there are people with yang energy who are introverted and retiring, there are also people with yin energy who are outgoing and extroverted. And by practicing self-care rituals that speak to your particular sign, energy, and governing body, you will reveal your true self and the balance of energy will be maintained.

Governing Elements

Each astrological sign has a governing element that defines their energy orientation and influences both the way the sign moves through the universe and relates to self-care. The elements are fire, earth, air, and water. All the signs in each element share certain characteristics, along with having their own sign-specific qualities:

* **Fire:** Fire signs are adventurous, bold, and energetic. They enjoy the heat and warm environments and look to the sun and fire as a means to recharge their depleted batteries. They're competitive, outgoing, and passionate. The fire signs are Aries, Leo, and Sagittarius.
* **Earth:** Earth signs all share a common love and tendency toward a practical, material, sensual, and economic orientation. The earth signs are Taurus, Virgo, and Capricorn.
* **Air:** Air is the most ephemeral element and those born under this element are thinkers, innovators, and communicators. The air signs are Gemini, Libra, and Aquarius.
* **Water:** Water signs are instinctual, compassionate, sensitive, and emotional. The water signs are Cancer, Scorpio, and Pisces.

Chapter 3 teaches you all about the ways your specific governing element influences and drives your connection to your cosmically harmonious self-care rituals, but it's important that you realize how important these elemental traits are to your self-care practice and to the activities that will help restore and reveal your true self.

Sign Qualities

Each of the astrological elements governs three signs. Each of these three signs is also given its own quality or mode, which corresponds to a different part of each season: the beginning, the middle, or the end.

* **Cardinal signs:** The cardinal signs initiate and lead in each season. Like something that is just starting out, they are actionable, enterprising, and assertive, and are born leaders. The cardinal signs are Aries, Cancer, Libra, and Capricorn.
* **Fixed signs:** The fixed signs come into play when the season is well established. They are definite, consistent, reliable, motivated by principles, and powerfully stubborn. The fixed signs are Taurus, Leo, Scorpio, and Aquarius.
* **Mutable signs:** The mutable signs come to the forefront when the seasons are changing. They are part of one season, but also part of the next. They are adaptable, versatile, and flexible. The mutable signs are Gemini, Virgo, Sagittarius, and Pisces.

Each of these qualities tells you a lot about yourself and who you are. They also give you invaluable information about the types of self-care rituals that your sign will find the most intuitive and helpful.

Ruling Planets

In addition to qualities and elements, each specific sign is ruled by a particular planet that lends its personality to those born under that sign. Again, these sign-specific traits give you valuable insight into the personality of the signs and the self-care rituals that may best rejuvenate them. The signs that correspond to each planet—and the ways that those planetary influences determine your self-care options—are as follows:

* **Aries:** Ruled by Mars, Aries is passionate, energetic, and determined.
* **Taurus:** Ruled by Venus, Taurus is sensual, romantic, and fertile.
* **Gemini:** Ruled by Mercury, Gemini is intellectual, changeable, and talkative.
* **Cancer:** Ruled by the Moon, Cancer is nostalgic, emotional, and home loving.
* **Leo:** Ruled by the Sun, Leo is fiery, dramatic, and confident.
* **Virgo:** Ruled by Mercury, Virgo is intellectual, analytical, and responsive.
* **Libra:** Ruled by Venus, Libra is beautiful, romantic, and graceful.
* **Scorpio:** Ruled by Mars and Pluto, Scorpio is intense, powerful, and magnetic.
* **Sagittarius:** Ruled by Jupiter, Sagittarius is optimistic, boundless, and larger than life.

* **Capricorn:** Ruled by Saturn, Capricorn is wise, patient, and disciplined.
* **Aquarius:** Ruled by Uranus, Aquarius is independent, unique, and eccentric.
* **Pisces:** Ruled by Neptune and Jupiter, Pisces is dreamy, sympathetic, and idealistic.

A Word on Sun Signs

When someone is a Leo, Aries, Sagittarius, or any of the other zodiac signs, it means that the sun was positioned in this constellation in the heavens when they were born. Your Sun sign is a dominant factor in defining your personality, your best self-care practices, and your soul nature. Every person also has the position of the Moon, Mercury, Venus, Mars, Jupiter, Saturn, Uranus, Neptune, and Pluto. These planets can be in any of the elements: fire signs, earth signs, air signs, or water signs. If you have your entire chart calculated by an astrologer or on an Internet site, you can see the whole picture and learn about all your elements. Someone born under Leo with many signs in another element will not be as concentrated in the fire element as someone with five or six planets in Leo. Someone born in Pisces with many signs in another element will not be as concentrated in the water element as someone with five or six planets in Pisces. And so on. Astrology is a complex system and has many shades of meaning. For our purposes, looking at the self-care practices designated by your Sun sign, or what most people consider *their* sign, will give you the information you need to move forward and find fulfillment and restoration.

CHAPTER 3

ESSENTIAL ELEMENTS: AIR

The air element is perhaps the most elusive element of the zodiac. Air is everywhere, invisible, and yet completely necessary for life. We are so sensitive to air that we even feel a momentary change in the currents around us or the amount of oxygen in our body.

In astrology, air is the third element of creation, preceded by earth and fire. The air signs (Gemini, Libra, and Aquarius) are the thinkers of the zodiac. Their dominion is mental—the realm of ideas and concepts. For example, you may have heard the saying that a person "builds castles in the air" or "has his head in the clouds." These statements are usually made as pejorative expressions, but for air signs they describe the essence of who they are. Air signs live in a world of both rational and intuitive thought. They are imaginative and dream, sometimes idealistically, of new and better ways to be, to think, and to communicate. Any self-care they do must reflect that disposition as well. Let's take a look at the mythological importance of air and its counterparts, the basic characteristics of the three air signs, and what they all have in common when it comes to self-care.

The Mythology of Air

In Greek mythology the legend of Icarus has a symbolic meaning with the air element. In this myth Icarus and his father, Daedalus, a talented Athenian craftsman responsible for building a labyrinth for King Minos to imprison the Minotaur, were themselves imprisoned in the labyrinth in Crete for crimes against the king. To escape the Minotaur, Daedalus fashioned wings of wax and feathers that he and his son could use to fly over the sea. Daedalus warned his son not to fly too near the sun as the heat would cause his wings to melt. But Icarus became enchanted by his freedom and flew too close to the sun. Soon, the wax melted and Icarus fell into the sea.

The lesson for the air signs in this myth is that going beyond sense and reason usually does not work out. In the case of Icarus, he followed his desire instead of his rational side, and ended up falling to his death. Ideas are wonderful—they are the foundation of many great creations. But for air signs, ideas are followed by the hard work of grounding them in physical reality. Self-care rituals that cater to both mind and heart are key for air signs, but balance and rationale are often paramount.

The Element of Air

Air signs are known for their curiosity, pursuit of knowledge, and keen ability to communicate. They delight in conversation and feel most passionate when they are confronting a dilemma of the mind straight on. But their grand ideas sometimes make them unpredictable. Because of this, they must be challenged in all parts of their lives. Doing the same thing over and over will just leave them bored. This goes for self-care as well. They need variety and different options for wellness activities, or they may not participate at all. Air signs are buoyant, perceptive, and inventive. For example, Gemini is expressive and always ready to entertain. Libra is gentle and will listen to a friend's troubles for hours. And Aquarius is ingenious, helping to solve problems with different approaches.

Astrological Symbols

The astrological symbols (also called the zodiacal symbols) of the air signs also give you hints as to how air signs move through the world. Each symbol ties back to the analytical, curious nature associated with air signs:

* Gemini is the Twins
* Libra is the Scales
* Aquarius is the Water Bearer

All these signs show intimate harmony with the cycles of the seasons and a personal connection with air. Gemini represents duality of the mind, and his symbol resembles the Roman numeral two. Libra brings balance with his scales of justice. And Aquarius represents positive movement and nourishment with waves of water or electricity. Each air sign's personality and subsequent approaches to self-care tie back to the qualities of these symbols.

Signs and Seasonal Modes

Each of the elements in astrology has a sign that corresponds to a different part of each season.

* **Fixed:** Aquarius is a fixed air sign. He rules in winter. The fixed signs are definite, motivated by principles, and powerfully stubborn.
* **Mutable:** Gemini is the first air sign and marks the end of spring and the beginning of summer. Gemini is called a mutable air sign because he ushers us from one season to the next. Mutable signs are changeable and flexible.
* **Cardinal:** Libra, the second air sign, occurs in autumn; he is the cardinal air sign because the autumn equinox occurs around Libra's time. The cardinal signs are leaders and action-oriented.

If you know your element and whether you are a cardinal, fixed, or mutable sign, you know a lot about yourself. This is invaluable for self-care and is reflected in the customized air sign self-care rituals found in Part 2.

Air Signs and Self-Care

When it comes to self-care, air signs must realize that they have a very sensitive nervous system. Not only do they react to changes in the weather and the "vibrations" around them in social situations, they also react to the power of words and ideas. Sometimes, they are not aware that their words can wound others, but they are always aware when someone says something hurtful to them. However, air signs are not a feeling sign, they are a thinking sign. They perceive that they are angry or hurt, but their feelings are expressed more in terms of the other person's actions, so they'll respond with "I thought that was rude," or "how unkind and cruel." Self-care must involve tapping into their emotions as well as the logic that precedes them.

Air signs are not oriented toward the physical. For instance, they know they have to eat and take care of their health, but the action comes second to thinking about it all. They can lose track of time and forget that they only had a croissant for breakfast! The first part of any self-care program for air signs is to understand the concept that self-care is a good thing to do for an easier and more productive life. Long-range thinking is an air sign specialty, so why not apply it to long-range self-care goals? This makes intuitive sense to air signs. In this way the most successful self-care activities should be interesting and involve an overall concept, such as "If I do this, I will learn some new ways of understanding myself and others," or "This is a new therapy that promises to eliminate my posture problem. I will check it out." Just doing something is not enough—air signs want to be sure of their reasons.

Repeating meaningless habits is a pitfall for air signs. If they get stuck in a rut, they'll ditch their self-care and run off to a party instead. Air signs are creative, and the same effort they exert for a nice dinner, social outing, story, or song should also apply to self-care. On the flip side, any activity or program that is cumbersome won't last long with air signs. If there is too much equipment to deal with or too much effort to get to that particular gym or hiking trail, the air sign just won't do it.

Air signs have an aesthetic sense in all aspects of their lives, which is why any self-care activity has to be effective as well as pleasing to the eye. For example, a diet plan must be tasty and involve food that is beautifully displayed. Those two qualities please air signs and will motivate them. The plan also has to be simple to follow. No elaborate timetables, just clear directions.

So now that you know what air signs need to practice self-care, let's look at each of the changeable characteristics of Gemini and how he can maintain his gifts.

CHAPTER 4

SELF-CARE FOR GEMINI

Dates: May 21–June 20
Element: Air
Polarity: Yang
Quality: Mutable
Symbol: Twins
Ruler: Mercury

Gemini is the first air sign of the zodiac. He is yang and a mutable sign, meaning that his sign rules while the season changes from spring to summer. And his personality is mutable or changeable as well—extremely changeable, in fact. Gemini is a dual sign and symbolizes the duality between the conscious mind and the divine universal mind. The tension between these two forces gives Gemini characteristics that resemble a split personality or, in some cases, a two-faced person.

This is not conscious duplicity on the part of Gemini. It is just Gemini exercising all parts of his mental faculties. In this way Gemini can be exhausting and frustrating to others, but he is usually so charming and witty that we feel glad for his company. Gemini's purpose in life is gathering different experiences and knowledge to further his mental and communication abilities.

Gemini's symbol, the Twins, is one of three human signs in the zodiac. It represents the human power of speech, thought, and communication. Using these skills, Gemini is always in the pursuit of his other half. In one legend from Greek mythology, the Twins were represented by the brothers Castor and Pollux. Castor was mortal, while Pollux was immortal. When Castor met an untimely death, Pollux was completely inconsolable. Zeus, ruler of the gods, pitied Pollux's grief and allowed him to live with his brother for six months of the year in the underworld. Another legend asserts that the two brothers never actually meet because when one is in heaven, the other is on earth, never to overlap.

The first legend explains Gemini's desire for unity, while the second explains the divisive impulse that is also native to Gemini. Gemini's quest and lifelong goal is to make peace with these opposing tendencies. Based on these traits, you can understand why Gemini has a reputation for going in two directions and changing his mind frequently. He is hard to pin down, which can be most obvious in intimate relationships.

Gemini is ruled by the planet Mercury, or Hermes in Greek. Statues depicting Mercury always include wings on his feet and a caduceus, a short staff with two entwined serpents and wings at the top, which he carries with him everywhere. Even today the caduceus is a symbol of the medical profession. The serpents represent life's healing energies, and the wings represent the messenger or physician who explains the best way of restoring health. Hermes was Zeus's messenger, or the messenger of the gods. It makes sense that Gemini is always busily gathering knowledge about self-care to give to us all.

Self-Care and Gemini

Intellectually, Gemini has no problem nurturing and taking care of his mental well-being. He is always looking into learning something new, whether that comes in the form of a lecture, a class, or a new book to read. It is in the physical realm where Gemini may need some guidance and help.

Gemini has a very sensitive nervous system that causes him to have a restless mind and body. He has "the monkey mind," as it is called in Eastern traditions, which scatters his thoughts and makes it hard to concentrate for long periods of time. His mind is so active that he often neglects his physical well-being. It's not unusual for Gemini to forget to eat or exercise because of his intellectual pursuits. He may not find self-care particularly interesting, so the best way to spark his passion is for him to begin researching information on diet, food, exercise, or activity. When he reads that such and such food or vitamin or immune-enhancing practice promotes good health in body, mind, and spirit, then Gemini is on board for self-care and delights in the results (as well as gaining more knowledge).

Gemini Rules the Lungs, Hands, and Shoulders

Gemini rules the lungs, hands, and shoulders. Note that there are two of each of these body parts. The most important of these body parts are the lungs and all parts of the respiratory system. Breathing well is a learned skill, one we have naturally as babies and children, but lose when the tensions of adulthood in life disrupt our well-being. This leads us to hold our breath and then, over time, our natural rhythm of breathing tightens. Mentally and spiritually, finding a breathing practice that calms the mind is essential for Gemini. This requires patience and practice. Gemini's mind is so active that he moves from thought to thought with lightning speed. Meditation, or slowing these thoughts, can be tough to accomplish. Because of this, meditating with sounds or chants is more likely to be successful for Gemini.

Gemini needs to relax his shoulders as much as possible. It may benefit Gemini to keep a yoga roll handy so he can lie on it and rest his neck and shoulders naturally. It may also be helpful for Gemini to do some shrugging exercises and shoulder rotations throughout the day to ensure that these body parts don't get stiff and his breathing doesn't become constricted. It's important for him to avoid propping the phone up with his left or right shoulder. Gemini loves to talk on the phone and be social, but if he props the receiver up against his shoulder, it can form a tension pattern throughout his shoulders and neck.

Turning to therapy or counseling is a great way for Gemini to practice psychological self-care, as it allows him to talk through all of his thoughts and ideas with a willing listener. However, Gemini is a thinking sign, not a feeling sign, and because of this, once Gemini gets his problem clear in his mind, he is not inclined to continue exploring the backstory of his life. He just enjoys the knowledge he's acquired, recognizes the benefits from the experience, and then moves on. Throughout his life he may try different therapies and work with a variety of therapists as the need arises, but it is typically only for a short period of time.

Sports and exercise are usually part of Gemini's self-care program. Gemini enjoys playing both team games and solo sports, depending on his mood. Sports like tennis, basketball, racquetball, badminton, and volleyball all require hand-eye coordination that

Gemini excels in. His muscles are usually long and flexible, and he does well in sports that require bursts of energy rather than endurance. Pure cardio is not usually interesting for Gemini unless he has a very jazzy soundtrack he can plug into. The repetitive motion of impact exercise is unpleasant to Gemini. He prefers to keep his eye on the ball and move freely. In addition, sports provide a social outlet for Gemini.

Dancing and singing along to music, or just repeating rhyming lyrics, is fun for Gemini. He is a natural mimic and loves wordplay. Karaoke must have been designed by a Gemini! Whatever Gemini does, he tries to make it amusing for himself and others. He's the member of the friend group that knows all the verses to camp songs. And he may even entertain by performing rap songs. It is the combo of rhythm and words that gets Gemini's system going.

Gemini and Self-Care Success

By nature, Gemini flees from boredom. If any activity or self-care practice is tedious or monotonous, Gemini will not stick to it, even if he knows he is doing something that is good for his overall well-being. He needs constant change to keep his mind stimulated. Because of this, the best approach to exercise for Gemini is to rotate activities so they do not become habitual. Having too many distractions is another pitfall for Gemini when it comes to self-care. If there are too many other interesting things going on in Gemini's life, he'll drop his self-care routine quickly. In addition, the more he speaks about an activity, the less he will do it. It is almost as if using energy to talk about something uses up the energy to do it. For Gemini it's better to just move into action.

Gemini needs socialization to really keep the ball rolling with self-care. For example, if Gemini partakes in a sport, it's a good idea for him to go out after the game for drinks to decompress with his teammates. This is a great opportunity for him to relive the glory of the game he just played, and plan for the next one.

If Gemini is in need of intellectual self-care, perhaps he can find a group to play chess with, or attend a lecture. Poetry readings, literary clubs, and book groups are also great Gemini self-care activities. All these activities feed Gemini's love of knowledge and words.

Gemini has a tendency to approach self-care with scattered efforts, which can become a hazard for his long-term wellness. Gemini also has wanderlust, and if he is traveling, good health and self-care may fall by the wayside. One way to get around this for Gemini is to locate a gym or spa wherever he goes. That way he can travel *and* keep his healthy habits intact at the same time. Two really is the magic number for all Gemini activities.

Blogging is a great option for Gemini, especially when he needs to track his health. If he finds he is struggling with keeping up with his self-care routine, maintaining a record of his self-care journey and then sharing tips with an Internet community can reinforce good personal self-care practices and spread the word to others. Gemini is not really concerned with accomplishing his self-care goals in measurable terms. The pleasure comes from communicating his hard work to others and giving helpful suggestions for their own journey. After all, Gemini is the messenger for us all!

Gemini is one of the most important zodiac signs, as he represents the opposition of the human and divine. Humanity may strive for the divine, but it must confront the narrower human nature first. Gemini doesn't necessarily have "the answer" on how humanity can save itself, but he is a messenger who will always communicate his thoughts and hopes for the holistic development of all people.

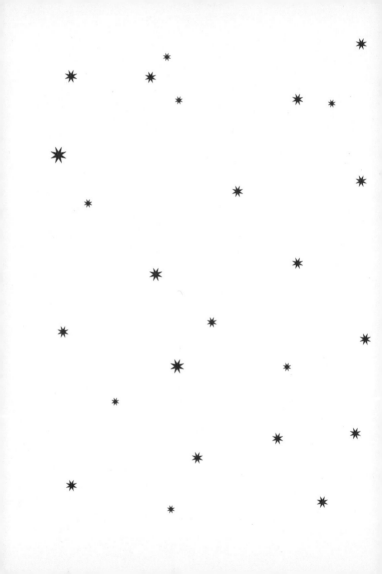

♊

PART 2

SELF-CARE
RITUALS
— FOR —
GEMINI

Add a Little Color

Gemini does not like to be confined. He wants to be free to express himself openly and without judgment. His personality is naturally colorful and buoyant, so he needs space to let those colors shine through. Encourage yourself to be creative and to express what's inside you through color. You can buy a large set of colored pencils and put them in a vase somewhere you can access easily when you feel the desire to draw something or write down your thoughts. Don't be afraid to mix and match the colors based on your mood!

Go Cloud-Watching

A ir signs are intellectual thinkers who excel at creative thought and problem-solving. But sometimes that can mean it's hard to turn off your racing mind. If you're having trouble figuring out the answer to a question, take care of yourself today by taking a well-deserved break to clear your mind. Need something else to focus on? Look up at the clouds. Take some time to lie back and watch the clouds move through the sky. You're sure to feel refreshed and will be able to look at any challenges with a fresh perspective.

Take a Whiff of Invigorating Scents

Air signs like Gemini can be invigorated by scents that inspire the mind and stimulate the body. If you aren't sure where to begin with aromatherapy, don't worry. Gemini benefits most from two common essences: peppermint and jasmine. Peppermint and jasmine can both help improve memory and raise alertness. Try adding the recommended amount of drops of one of these essential oils to an appropriate carrier oil for topical use (diluting according to instructions), or buy an essential oil diffuser that will spread one of these scents all around your home when you are in need of a little brain boost.

Head to the Swimming Pool

———————

I t may come as a surprise, but swimming is actually great for air signs. Air signs are known for loving to think about problems from every angle, but sometimes it's important to have a mental break. With swimming you'll need to focus on mastering each movement and maintaining fluid motions, so it's a great way to calm your mind. Allow yourself to relax and feel restored as you take a break from your worries.

Swimming is also a great way for air signs to get some exercise. Regular swim sessions will help you build lung power and stamina. So instead of your regular workout, head to your local pool and do some laps.

Do a Duet

Karaoke, anyone? Gemini loves to do everything in twos, especially when it comes to entertaining and showing off his many talents. When you are feeling the need to let loose and connect with others, try hitting up a local karaoke night with a group of friends. But instead of just getting up on stage alone, test out your vocal prowess by singing a duet with a trusted confidant or even a stranger.

Can't carry a tune, Gemini? Don't worry. Just listening to duets can soothe your soul. The intense creative connection between two people is inspiring and will remind you of how powerful your voice is when it is joined by others.

Use Writing Prompts

Air signs are often creative and great at expression. Why not try channeling those skills into some writing? Some well-known authors such as Shel Silverstein, Oscar Wilde, Charles Dickens, and Judy Blume were able to channel their air sign qualities into incredible literary works—maybe you can too!

Not sure where to start? Writing prompts are a great way to boost your creativity and give you the kind of challenge you love. Look for a writing prompt book at your local library, or check out different social media communities for ideas to help you get started.

Embrace Spring

S pring is a time of rebirth and renewal. The flowers are blooming, the bees are buzzing, and the leaves are filling the once barren trees. Gemini thrives on the fresh energy of spring and promise of new beginnings. Hold on to that feeling year-round by surrounding yourself with springtime colors at all times. Everything from pale blue to soft green and light yellow will instantly remind you of that sweet, spring air. These are colors that suggest a spring breeze and will immediately revitalize your heart and soul.

Unplug Before Bed

———————————

E ven the most communicative air sign will sometimes need a break to feel refreshed and reenergized after a long day. Getting a good night's sleep will also help rejuvenate your nervous system, so do whatever you can to ensure pleasant dreams and a restful evening.

A good first step is to unplug from social media before heading to bed, and, if possible, keep technology out of the bedroom entirely. Stop scrolling through social media and give yourself a break from your tablet or computer. Minimize your information input by avoiding TV—especially news programs— before bedtime. If possible you can even eliminate clocks from your bedroom for a more peaceful sleep.

Breathe Deep

Gemini rules the lungs, so it's important he takes special care with the air he breathes. In winter that air becomes dry and harsh. It can make your skin scaly and cracked, and cause congestion in your lungs and nose. When the temperature starts to plummet and you start feeling a little tickle in your throat, turn to lemon eucalyptus to keep you breathing easy. You can use a lemon eucalyptus aromatherapy spray mist, or diffuse lemon eucalyptus essential oil in an oil diffuser, to permeate the air with this calming scent, cooling your lungs and acting as an anti-inflammatory agent against viruses. Just a little will do!

Whistle Your Way Through Chores

Vacuuming or washing dishes might not be your favorite activity, but sometimes those boring chores simply need to get done. Intellectual air signs need some kind of fun activity to keep the mind otherwise occupied, especially when faced with a few hours of dusting and sweeping. Try whistling or humming while doing chores. It'll help keep your brain focused as you work, and may be a good creative outlet if you're especially interested in music. You'll also help strengthen your lungs—all that humming is a mini-breathing exercise!

Create the Perfect Work Space

Air signs are intellectual problem-solvers with great critical-thinking skills. Make sure your work space is ready! Whether you work at home or spend your days in a professional office, it's important to make sure you create a productive work space. Start with your chair so you're comfortable and able to focus. Your chair should be lightweight and on rollers so you can move around easily. Your spontaneous nature will appreciate the ease with which you can shift around and collaborate with your coworkers.

If you work around a lot of computers and technical equipment, ask an expert about setting up a portable ionizer to help neutralize their electromagnetic vibrations. It will help improve the air quality and keep you feeling your best.

Identify Bird Calls

Turn to nature to re-center your spirit, Gemini. Start by waking up early in the morning and going for a short walk, focusing on all the different birds singing in the trees. Each bird has their own special call. Do some research online about birds in your area and what their calls sound like. Each time you go out for a walk, try and identify which bird you hear. You may even consider recording their songs on your phone to play back later. As a Gemini you have a special affinity for birds. A bird's songs can lift your mood and get you ready to take on the day. Embrace your intrinsic connection with these animals.

Carry a Crystal

The energy in a crystal can have lasting effects on your mood and spirit. For example, rose quartz can increase loving feelings, amethyst provides spiritual protection, and onyx promotes balance and healing. Gemini benefits most from pale tourmaline, a green stone that enhances courage, strength, and vitality. Carrying tourmaline, or other appropriate crystals, is good for Gemini. Crystals are grounding, which is important for air signs.

Keep it in your left pocket, or near your bed at night. When you are feeling uneasy or like you need a boost of bravery, hold it in your palm and squeeze. Depending on your crystal, you can also cleanse it by leaving it out in the moonlight or rinsing it in cold water.

Learn about Aikido

Inspired by various martial arts techniques, aikido is more than fighting—it's really about self-development, focus, peace, and balance. Participants can use their practice to find what they need, whether that's a healthy workout or a focus on spirituality. To get started, look for beginners' classes in your area or check on online course offerings for a better idea of what to expect before signing up.

Perfect for air signs, aikido is a powerful and beautiful martial art. Since air signs may enjoy opportunities for self-improvement and collaboration, aikido can be a great way to focus your overactive mind. You'll appreciate the graceful movements that will remind you of your air-like qualities.

Become a Social Butterfly

Connection is your strong suit, so head out to events, get-togethers, and parties to meet new people. Social events bring out the best in air signs, who are in their element when surrounded by engaging conversation and interesting ideas. Try attending a reading at your local bookstore, checking out the speakers at a nearby college, or simply following your friends to a party. Socializing with different types of people comes naturally to air signs, so you may find your friend group growing rapidly in ways you never expected. You'll increase your own knowledge of the world by meeting other people, so don't be afraid to let your natural social butterfly tendencies shine!

Take a Historical Trip

Are you in need of a vacation, Gemini? Recharge your battery by indulging in one of history's greatest destinations: Egypt. Located in the north-eastern part of Africa, Egypt boasts one of humanity's greatest marvels, the Great Pyramid of Giza, constructed sometime between 2589 and 2566 B.C. The Great Pyramid is the oldest of the Seven Wonders of the Ancient World, with a rich past that you don't need to be a history buff to appreciate.

If you can't make the trip, look for ways to experience history without going too far. Many Geminis have had past lives as scribes. You could have inhabited one of those souls at one point in time. If you can, visit a museum with papyrus scrolls and revel in their fragility and beauty.

Record Your Ideas

Air signs are creative and often have a lot of ideas. Those ideas may be interesting and worth exploring in more detail, but they can sometimes require a little more thought than you're able to give in the moment. So give yourself an outlet to brainstorm and release those ideas in a constructive manner by writing everything down and keeping a record of your ideas—no matter how big or small they seem. You may consider keeping a journal and taking some time every day to record your thoughts, or you may just want to jot down your notes on your smartphone as they come to you.

Keep an eye out for patterns in your thinking—they might help reveal worries or build on broader ideas you didn't even realize you had.

Enjoy Some Cotton Candy

No summer is complete without the pink and blue sugar clouds known as cotton candy. Don't be fooled! Cotton candy is not just for kids. It's a fun, airy treat that will bring out your playful side. Plus, it's delicious.

Reconnecting with your inner child is important for air signs. Taking time to do something you haven't done since you were young is a great way to lift your spirit and shuffle off adult responsibilities. This is especially vital for Gemini. You need to feel free. While it may seem basic, a simple bag of cotton candy allows Gemini to reconnect with his most basic wants and desires without fear of judgment. So dig in! No regrets...

Keep Your Bedroom Airy

Gemini loves feeling air moving around him. It gives him the impression of being open and unrestrained, like he can take on anything. As an air sign, you need to feel air flow in your home or you might begin to feel claustrophobic. Try adding a few fans to your bedroom to keep the airflow moving freely. You may even consider hanging sheer or gauze curtains that move easily in the breeze. Seeing them sway will make you feel lighter and more hopeful. This is especially important in your bedroom, the last place you see before you sleep and the first you see when you wake.

If you want to lighten the energy in your home, especially your bedroom, consider smudging with white sage. Sage is an ancient herb that can cleanse negative energy from your home and promote positivity. Simply light a sage bundle in a fireproof dish, blow out, and let the smoke cleanse the area. Be sure to take proper precautions when using any flammable substance.

Listen to Choir Music

L istening to music can be a soothing, relaxing
experience for a weary Gemini. That's because
when you listen to music, your brain releases dopamine,
a "feel-good" neurotransmitter, increasing feelings of
happiness. It also decreases the amount of cortisol, or
stress hormone, in your body. Gemini is drawn to choir
music. In fact, the more voices involved the better!
Next time your nerves are frayed and you need to
unwind, try listening to a famous choir or orchestra.
Allow your mind to wander as you listen to the
different voices working together to create beauty
and harmony.

Read Poetry

Reading poetry is a wonderful way for Gemini to get in touch with his emotional side. As an air sign, you have a strong connection to the mind. You are a wordsmith. You learn quickly and thrive on exchanging ideas with others. Challenge your mind and your creative side by reading poetry of your choosing: anything from classical to modern. Look for symbolism within the poem. What kinds of poetic devices does the poet use? Maybe they are partial to similes and streams of consciousness. Or maybe they prefer rhyming schemes instead. Appreciate the images each word evokes in your mind, and the feelings that emerge in your heart.

Drink Valerian Tea

After a long day there's nothing quite like settling into bed with a nice warm cup of tea. Every tea has a different effect on the body, though, so make sure you choose the right one for the right moment. For example, if you are looking for one that will calm your nerves and promote sleep, ask your doctor (who is familiar with your health and medications) about valerian tea. Valerian is derived from the valerian plant, native to both Europe and Asia. It is claimed to have a soothing effect on the nervous system, one of the body systems Gemini rules, so it's a perfect fit for the stressed-out Gemini.

Tell a Story

Gemini is a natural storyteller. You are a gifted communicator who can adapt easily to any situation. This means you can create a story at the drop of a hat without any stress. Use your skills for good and start a storytelling group for children in your local neighborhood. Not only will this give you the chance to flex your creative muscles, but the kids will love every second. It's a low-tech form of entertainment that will never go out of style. If you aren't sure how to get started, check with your local library about putting together a group.

Get Some Fresh Air

———————————

Here's an easy way for air signs to take care of themselves: head outside to get some fresh air! Air signs truly value freedom and openness, so make sure to break up your day by spending some time outside. Take your morning coffee out to your porch, enjoy a book outside, or spend some time outdoors during the evenings and weekends. Choose to walk instead of drive wherever possible—not only will you feel healthier and more refreshed, but the environment will thank you as well!

"Vitamin O"—oxygen—is one of the most important factors to keep an air sign feeling revitalized and healthy.

Ride a Tandem Bike

Gemini will forever be looking for his other half. Because of this, he is drawn to activities that are meant specifically for two people, where he can connect and laugh without a lot of distraction. Embrace your carefree side and rent a tandem bike with a family member or trusted friend. You'll need to work together in order to keep the bike in motion. Luckily, Gemini shines in situations that require communication. Don't be discouraged if you wobble or start to tip over while you get the hang of the bike. Trust your partner and your own abilities, and you'll be peddling like a pro in no time.

Embrace Traditional Communication

Keeping in touch with friends and family is important for Gemini. Modern forms of communication such as texting and email have their perks, but they lack intimacy and personality. To remedy this, indulge in fine stationery and write notes to friends with a fountain pen. Even just a short note saying hello, and that you are thinking of the person, can have a profound impact on their mood. Your handwriting is unique to you, so it inherently communicates more than computer print. In addition, writing letters by hand can be a therapeutic act for Gemini. He is an expert communicator, after all, and needs the proper outlet to share his talent.

Support Clean Air

The environment is important to everyone, and air pollution is a cause any air sign can really get behind. It's important to take care of your health, and air signs will instinctually gravitate toward clean air as a way to keep their bodies strong, healthy, and happy.

Get involved in the movement for clean air! Do some research to learn about particular causes you'd like to support, like wind farms or other alternative energies. Donate to major clean air groups to help them fund their important work. Find out what programs exist in your area where you can volunteer your time. Air signs are great communicators, so volunteer your skills to help get the word out on clean air!

Repeat a Mantra

Gemini is ruled by the planet Mercury, which, according to mythology, was named for the messenger of the gods. Stories go that Mercury carried information from one level of existence to another, so it's no wonder Gemini is so good at communicating. It's an integral part of your astrological makeup. To capitalize on your strength, repeat the mantra "Words have power." Do this whenever you are feeling lost or overwhelmed. Find power in words and communication. It may help you re-center your mind and stay grounded.

Get a Pet Parakeet

Owning a pet is a rewarding experience, one that can help Gemini become more dependable, vulnerable, and responsible. If you've never had a pet before, it is best to start small. Because of your natural affinity for birds, parakeets are perfect Gemini pets. Not only are they low-maintenance, but they are beautiful, and their chirp is sweet and calming. Just make sure to get expert advice on adopting (and properly caring for) a parakeet from a local animal shelter before you commit. Also known as a budgie, parakeets are part of the parrot family, and are entertaining and social, and can sometimes be quite talkative. Kind of like you, Gemini.

Visit a Bookstore

Books can transport us into other worlds with just the turn of a page. Indulge your innate curiosity, Gemini. Take some time to explore a local secondhand bookstore one afternoon. Walk the aisles and touch each book's spine. Flip through the pages and look for old notes from previous owners. What's the oldest book you can find hidden on the shelves? Buy a book you've never heard of before. Listen to that intuitive voice inside guiding you along to help you find the perfect new addition to your home library.

Keep In Touch with Friends

Air signs are great at intercommunication, and it's important for their well-being to have that social interaction throughout their lives. Other signs though? Not so much. Before you get upset that you haven't heard from your friends in a while, try making the first move and reaching out. Send a quick text to a friend you haven't heard from in a while. Give your best friend a call, even if you only want to say hello. Reconnect with old friends over social media, or even send an email to let someone know you're thinking of them.

With our busy lives, people sometimes need reminders to keep in touch, and air signs are the perfect ones to take that step!

Pop Some Popcorn!

Popcorn is the perfect snack for hungry Gemini. It's light, fun, and simple to make, so it fits your personality and your schedule. While buying microwaveable bags of popcorn is the quickest way to enjoy your snack, consider buying a hot air popper instead. As an air sign, you'll love how quickly your favorite element can turn those tiny kernels into fluffy popcorn. Try seasoning your popcorn with various unusual ingredients to up the fun factor: anything from garlic salt to caramel drizzle, chocolate sauce, or white cheddar cheese. Your imagination is your only limit.

Learn a Foreign Language

Air signs are all about the exchange of information. It's important to them that they be able to get the word out and share their thoughts with others. Talking with new people helps you feel revitalized, so expand your communication skills by learning a foreign language. Try taking a course at your local community college or checking out one of the many apps and online programs to help you develop your skills. You may even consider planning a trip to the country that speaks that language. You'll get first-hand experience practicing your new skills and likely make new friends in the process!

Head Out on an Adventure

Air signs have an adventurous side, and you're known among your friends for being fun and spontaneous. If you're feeling a little bored lately, seek out some new experiences to recharge yourself and give you the excitement you need. Go for something a little unexpected with some wild (but still air-themed!) fun. Take a ride in a hot-air balloon to view your home from an entirely new perspective. Take a class to learn how to swing high on a trapeze for a unique workout. Or head out for a weekend away from home to learn kitesurfing from an expert. Give yourself the boost you need to keep your energy up!

Practice Origami

———————

Origami is the art of folding paper that is often associated with ancient Japanese culture. The ultimate objective is to transform a small, flat sheet of paper into a beautiful structure. It is a practice of patience and precision, both perfect goals for Gemini.

Buy a collection of origami paper, and learn how to get started by either researching online or picking up a book at your local bookstore. Don't try to make an origami piece that is too complicated too soon. Start with a simple shape, like a butterfly or fish, and work your way up to more complicated structures, like cranes. Ease into this craft, and enjoy how light, airy, and therapeutic it can be.

Try a Challenging Yoga Pose

Yoga is a wonderful practice for Gemini. It can help you tone your physical muscles as well as your mental muscles. Gemini often needs space to take a break and focus on himself, shutting out the outside world and all the stress that comes with it. Yoga can do just that, while teaching you patience, self-love, and commitment.

If you haven't tried yoga yet, look for local beginners' classes that can help you get started. If you are already a yoga veteran, challenge yourself by trying a Shoulderstand Pose. Gemini rules the shoulders, so you already have an intrinsic connection to these parts of your body. You'll need expert balance to do this pose, so make sure to practice this with your yoga instructor for technique guidance. They will guide you on where to focus your power and strength during the pose and help keep you upright and safe while you get the hang of it.

Take a Deep Breath

Air signs have highly tuned nervous systems, so certain breathing exercises can help you stay calm and relaxed. For a simple breathing technique you can employ anywhere, start by counting up from one to ten on an exhale. Then try counting down from ten to one as you inhale. You may find it helpful to close your eyes or put your hands on your stomach or chest to feel yourself breathing. Check out online resources or apps for alternate techniques. Whenever you're feeling a little stressed, take a moment to focus on yourself and your breathing.

Satisfy Your Curiosity

As an air sign, you are always connected to your mind, Gemini. You seek out mental stimulation, looking for your next great challenge. You have endless curiosity to explore different places, ideas, and people. Don't let your curiosity go unsatisfied. Maintain a list of things you want to know more about, and keep adding to it as often as possible. It can include anything that sparks your interest—from history to science or art. Then read about and research these topics. Go to the library, ask questions, and keep exploring!

Become Your Own Writing Prompt

As a Gemini, you love to share your ideas and thoughts with the world. You are articulate and insightful, and never back down when it comes to expressing your opinions—the perfect combination of traits for a master communicator. While you are already good at talking, take your communication skills to the next level by trying out a few personal writing prompts.

Every morning, think of a sentence and write it down in your journal. That evening, read the sentence and just start writing what comes to mind. This approach suits the dual way that Gemini approaches things. Your thoughts in the morning will be different than your thoughts at night. This is a great way to express your creativity privately; though feel free to share your writing with others if you feel comfortable.

Avoid Negative Conversation Overload

A ir signs are social and love to talk with other people. Since words are so important, air signs are also great at listening. But remember this: don't let yourself get burned out by tuning into negative conversations that don't involve you. Air signs can pick up other people's vibrations and energies through words, which can sometimes lead to a mental overload. Take a break and step away from the conversation, head outside for some fresh air, or redirect your focus toward something less draining and more relevant for you.

Find a Double Terminated Crystal

Double terminated crystals are unique stones that allow energy to flow in multiple directions through them. A double terminated crystal has two points, on opposite sides of the crystal. Your crystal may be diamond shaped if it has double termination points. Seek out these rare crystals for their open energy flow. Meditate with them to help clear any negative thoughts and emotions. The two points of a double terminated crystal are perfect for Gemini's dual mind.

Look for double terminated aquamarine crystals and clear quartz in particular. Aquamarine crystals invoke the healing power of the ocean, while clear quartz symbolizes purity. These are beneficial for a calming meditation and continued mental clarity.

Keep Your Windows Open

Your home should be a place for you to relax, recharge, and reconnect with yourself. So make sure to pay homage to your air sign qualities in your home décor. Whether you live in a house or apartment, you'll be happiest and most comfortable with lots of windows that open. Try to keep your windows open all year long, especially after a cold spell or heat wave. Even if you have central air or heat, it can be helpful to keep just one window open. Changing the air currents changes the energy in your home, so be sure to let fresh air and positive energy flow throughout your living space.

Read a Book

A ir signs love learning, communication, and the written word, so it makes sense that they'd also be interested in reading. If there's a book you've been dying to read or a magazine article that caught your eye, take some time for yourself and spend it reading, even if you only get to finish a couple of pages.

Not sure what you want to read? Head to your local library to check out some of the selections there. Look for a well-known classic like *Don Quixote* by Cervantes (a fellow air sign!), or try something brand-new and trendy. Still not sure where to start? Ask your librarian for a recommendation and start a conversation about some awesome books!

Get a Manicure

_____

Gemini rules the hands, so it is important to keep them in good shape. After all, we use them for pretty much everything. If your nails are in need of some TLC, schedule a manicure to restore them to their natural state. While a basic manicure is wonderful, splurging on a more luxurious treatment can really increase your hand health. A long hand massage can improve circulation in your hands and arms, making your skin glow. You may also consider asking about a paraffin wax treatment for your hands. The warm wax coats your hands in hydration, leaving your skin supple and soft.

Try to get a manicure at least once a month for maintenance. Your hands will thank you!

Make a To-Do List

Thought is so important to Gemini that he can easily become scattered with his thinking. You spend a lot of time in your mind assessing things and trying to understand the world around you. It's one of your best traits, though it can lead to confusion sometimes. Instead of letting your thoughts and grand plans get away from you, write them down on a to-do list.

Gemini is so restless that he often lacks staying power for projects, which means you probably have a few half-finished creations around you at all times. Start completing the tasks on your list, and check each one off as you do. This will give you a sense of accomplishment. Use that feeling as motivation to work your way down your list.

Enjoy Some Green Tea

Air signs are curious and great at solving problems—but that can also mean that they're chronic overthinkers as well. Give yourself a restorative break to clear your mind and reframe your mind-set. Not sure how to begin? Try making it a habit to drink a peaceful cup of green tea every day; mix it up with some fruit-flavored or jasmine green teas for a little variety. Use your daily cup of tea as a chance to clear your mind and take a break from worrying about anything stressful in your life. (If you have health problems or are on medication, check with your doctor first.)

Afterward, you're sure to find you feel more relaxed and rejuvenated, and ready to take on any challenges that come your way. Bring your tea outside for the added benefit of a little fresh air on your break!

Dine Alfresco

Remember, fresh air is vital for air signs, so it's important to reclaim that outdoor time for yourself. Free-spirited air signs appreciate a little spontaneous fun; try to be creative about how you find that time. For example, why not eat outdoors? Whether you're spending the day at the beach or boardwalk, or going on a picnic in the park, enjoying a healthy meal outdoors can be great for your physical and mental well-being. If you don't have time for an all-day event, you can still head outdoors by asking to be seated outside at a restaurant or even bringing a home-cooked meal out onto your own patio or deck.

Flavor with Fennel

One of the best spices that an inventive Gemini chef can use in his kitchen is fennel. Fennel is a Gemini-ruled spice that comes from the carrot family, and it can give the food you are cooking a light, herbal taste. Fennel has been used as a healing herb for centuries, helping prevent anemia, ease indigestion, and regulate blood pressure. Fennel is also a great source of fiber, potassium, folate, vitamin C, vitamin B_6, and phytonutrient content. It lowers cholesterol, too, so adding just a bit of it to your favorite meals is a wonderful way to support your heart health.

Tap Into Your Inner Child

———————

While Gemini spends a lot of time in his mind, sometimes he needs to break free and do something completely unexpected. One of the best ways to let loose is to channel your childhood by revisiting some of your favorite pastimes. Think of activities such as skipping rope and going on a swing. These actions get you moving and your body into the air. You may even remember some of your favorite jump rope rhymes you can test out, which stimulates your mind as well. Don't be afraid to let your inner child have some fun! It's a great way for a run-down Gemini to refuel when adult responsibilities become a bit too much.

Grow Purifying Houseplants

Did you know that plants can help purify the air around you? Try bringing some houseplants into your home to help improve the air quality. English ivy, bamboo palm, and peace lilies are all beautiful houseplants that will help remove airborne toxins from your home. There are plenty of other options, however, so do some research to see what will grow well in your home. Warning, though, some plants are poisonous to house pets, so make sure to take the needs of your furry friends into consideration as well. Choose the plants that work best for you, and, as an air sign, you will feel your best and most balanced around these natural air purifiers.

Keep Communication Open

Even great communicators like air signs can have disagreements with friends and family members. But you're likely to feel unbalanced when conflict causes the lines of communication to be closed. So clear the air and reopen those lines. It's important to remember not to hold onto grudges, so if you have any negative feelings, try to let them go and approach the conversation with a positive attitude. Do your best to be patient and flexible with the other person—remember, not everyone is as good at expression as you are! Work together to get back in balance and bring your relationships to a happier state.

Host a Game Night

———————

Air signs love to be social, and that social interaction is all they need to spark some happiness and excitement into their everyday lives! You're likely well known for being great company, so grab some snacks, pull out your favorite games, and invite some friends over for game night! Some friendly competition and interesting conversations will help you reconnect with friends you haven't seen in a while.

For some added air sign fun, look for word-based games that will play to your language-loving strengths. Scrabble, Boggle, and Bananagrams are all popular options, but there are plenty of lesser known variations that you might enjoy.

Listen to Wind Instruments

When it comes to music, wind instruments get a bad rap. They aren't as cool as the big string and percussion instruments like the guitar, piano, and drums, but the music they create is just as compelling. Wind is especially important to Gemini, as an air sign, so it is only natural you would have a positive response to instruments like flutes, clarinets, and saxophones. Try listening to chamber music with a special focus on wind instruments. Chamber music is composed using only a few instruments, so it is not as robust as orchestral music, making it more intimate and calming.

Record Your Thoughts

Do you ever feel like you have so many thoughts running through your mind at one time that you can't keep everything straight? Don't worry; this is typical for Gemini. Your mind is often very active, jumping from one idea to the next. Try to ease the chaos by recording your thoughts as voice memos. You can just say what's on your mind, or even record inspiring thoughts for yourself to listen to at a later time. Try reciting encouraging quotes that you've always loved, or giving yourself a little pep talk. You may feel silly talking to yourself at first, but you are your own best advocate and cheerleader!

Stretch Your Shoulders

Gemini rules over the shoulders, so he tends to carry most of his stress in that area as well. If you have problems with your shoulder muscles, you may feel tightness or soreness from your upper middle back into your neck. To ease this tension, try a few simple shoulder stretches. Start with some shoulder rolls. Curve your shoulders forward, and then roll them up and back. Repeat a few times throughout the day. Another option is simple chin retractions. Sit up straight and pull your chin backward, toward the neck, and then bring it back to a neutral position. If your shoulder pain doesn't resolve, it's always a good idea to see your doctor.

Take Yourself to the Movies

A ir signs love learning about new ideas, and a great way to do so is to head to the movies. Treat yourself to a couple of hours of comfortable seating, buttery popcorn, and an interesting new movie. You might try checking out a documentary or something that's particularly thought-provoking.

Although it's always fun to bring friends to the movie theater, you might consider making the occasional trip alone. Air signs appreciate the opportunity to think deeply about things they've learned. Enjoy the time alone to really analyze and fully process the movie you've just seen.

Hang Out in a Hammock

As an air sign, it's important for you to get outside and get some fresh air. One great way to unwind and recharge outside is to relax in a hammock. Enjoy rocking in the breeze and give yourself permission to take a quick mental break. You can chat with friends nearby or spend some time by yourself, appreciating the nature around you. You should even feel free to close your eyes and take a little nap—you'll feel incredibly relaxed when you wake up! But if you're still in need of some mental stimulation to distract yourself, bring a book with you and take a little time to read. Your intellectual side will thank you!

Start a Book Club

Because Gemini rules over the mind, you hold a special love for words and knowledge. You also love sharing your ideas with others. Try putting both of these passions together by joining or starting a book club. Start by seeing if any of your friends are already part of a book club, and, if they aren't, whether they'd like to start one with you. A book club is a great outlet for curious Gemini. Not only will being part of a book club give you a chance to be social, but you'll also exchange ideas and learn something new.

Clear Space in Your Home

Air signs may seem like they're in constant motion. And that's certainly true of their minds, which are often off and running to solve whatever problems come their way. Yet sometimes air signs can get thrown off—both physically and mentally—by stagnant air in their home.

If you start feeling stuck or out of balance, get rid of anything old or musty in your home or apartment. Also consider rearranging the furniture, as moving furniture allows the air to circulate more easily through your living spaces. Your thoughts will mimic the newly refreshed space and be able to flow more freely.

Listen to a TED Talk

There's always something new to learn, as long as you are open to it. Gemini knows this better than anyone else. His eagerness to acquire new knowledge is one of his most defining characteristics. But it's not easy satisfying this drive in new and exciting ways. There are only so many books you can read, movies you can watch, and websites you can frequent. To satiate your cravings for knowledge, try listening to a TED Talk. TED Talks are lectures, given by experts in their field, recorded, and streamed online. There are thousands of topics to choose from, and you may even pick up some public-speaking tips!

Analyze Your Handwriting

With the air signs' interest in communication, they're likely to appreciate the importance of writing and may be very interested in what they can learn from their own handwriting. Your handwriting could be an important key to revealing some interesting aspects of your personality. Things like the slant, size, and thickness of your letters can be important, so have your handwriting analyzed! For instance, did you know that large letters indicate a big personality? If your handwriting slants to the right, you might like to meet new people. Learn some basic handwriting analysis tricks and practice your new skills with your friends to see if you can get to know them better!

Think First, Speak Second

———————

Your verbal dexterity as an air sign can sometimes get you into hot water if you aren't careful, Gemini. You are so adept with words and thought, you may not filter what's in your head before it comes out of your mouth. This can lead to insensitive and harsh speech. You may not mean to cause harm or to hurt someone with your words, but if you don't stop and think about what you are going to say before you say it, you run the risk of doing serious damage. Before you say something, pause for 1–2 seconds, and think about the impact your statement may make. If you have any doubt that it may hurt someone, rephrase it or keep it in your mind.

Travel the World

———————————

Air signs may seem as if they're always on the move, so think about places you might like to visit to actually get yourself moving. It's always a good idea to have a trip planned for the near future. You don't have to go far or plan an extensive, expensive vacation, but a nice weekend away or a few nights in a place you've always wanted to visit can give you something to look forward to and keep your energy high. Try visiting someplace peaceful to give yourself a chance to recharge, or research places you could visit to add an intellectual element to your next trip, like cities with interesting museums or historical monuments. Your adventurous free spirit will appreciate the change of scenery.

Start a Collection

_____

You may have noticed that your natural curiosity drives you to accumulate new information whenever you can. Have you ever just needed the answer to whatever question is plaguing you immediately? That's because Gemini loves to learn.

One of the best ways to learn about something new is to start a collection. It doesn't matter what you collect; though, if you are unsure where to begin, start by picking something that relates to Gemini's personality. For instance, you could collect objects like vintage telephones (Gemini likes gadgets that keep people in touch), old dictionaries and encyclopedias (Gemini is also curious about language), or pens (Gemini likes all communication tools). The more you add to your collection, the more information you'll acquire.

Write a Blog

_____

You've accumulated a lot of knowledge over the years, Gemini. It's time to share what you've learned with others. Starting a blog is the perfect way for you to pinpoint a topic you are drawn to and share that love with the world. Start by picking a topic you are knowledgeable and passionate about. Don't worry if it seems too niche—the Internet is a wide expanse; someone will want to learn what you know. Once you have an idea in mind, just start writing! Try to keep your blog up-to-date and offer your readers new content as often as possible.

Continue Your Education

A ir signs are the intellectuals of the zodiac and are always looking to learn something new. Continue your education by pursuing an advanced degree. By doing so, you'll be practicing good mental self-care through fully engaging in an intellectual pursuit. However, you might also find some practical benefits to continuing your education. By pursuing a degree in your field, you may discover that you're better qualified for a different position in your company. Or, if you choose to expand your horizons and go for a new degree in an entirely different field, you might be able to move into a new dream job.

Stop Gossiping

_____

Because air signs are so great at communication, people really enjoy talking to them. That can be great news—you love speaking to and learning from a lot of people—but you need to be careful with everything you learn. People will often feel comfortable sharing their personal issues with you, and it's up to you to be respectful of that. Avoid gossiping, and don't share anyone's personal information without their permission. For someone as social as you are, it's important that you keep your friendships in good shape. Your friends trust you, so remember to honor their feelings to keep your relationships going strong.

Plan a Trip with Friends

Being social is important to Gemini. He often feels most comfortable and relaxed when he is in a group setting, as long as the group is made up of trusted friends and family. Soothe your soul by taking a vacation with a group of friends. Being in a new place with valued friends can nurture Gemini's curious side. Go somewhere warm so you can all be outside together in nature, enjoying the fresh air. Plan group outings that challenge you physically and mentally. Most of all, laugh together and share your thoughts and emotions. Create memories that will last a lifetime.

Try Mindful Breathing

———————————

Our breath is an extension of our souls. Learning how he can control his breathing can help a weary Gemini focus his mind and calm his body. Another way to calm your body is to try progressive relaxation. Slowly tighten each part of your body for a few seconds, and then release it. Start with your head and work your way down, touching on each muscle group. When you reach your toes, your muscles should feel relaxed and warm.

You can increase your relaxation by also focusing on your breathing during this time. Breathe in slowly, counting to three, hold your breath, counting to three, and then release slowly, counting to three again.

Try doing these exercises in the morning to center yourself. They may help you focus your thoughts before the day begins, which is important since Gemini is a go-go-go personality.

Decorate with Wind Chimes

A ir signs can sometimes have the energy of a powerful wind with their free-spirited natures. Why not bring that inspiration into your home décor? Try putting some wind chimes on your porch, by the entrance to your home, or somewhere else where you'll be able to hear them often. If you live in an apartment, putting your chimes near a window should be enough to get them ringing.

Putting a wind chime in your home can be a great way to remind yourself of some of your great air sign qualities. Every time you hear it ringing, you'll be reminded of your fun, adventurous side!

Sign Up for a Writing Course

Air signs are known for being great at expression and deep thinking. So why not expand your communication skills by taking a writing course? Although it may seem intimidating to put all your thoughts onto paper, you may be surprised to find you have a hidden writing talent! The good news is, writing classes span a variety of areas from fiction and poetry to screenwriting and presentation development. You're sure to find something that fits your interests!

You may find that you thrive in a social environment, like a class at a local college, where you can share your ideas with your classmates and develop your skills together. But if you're feeling a little shy about sharing your first writing attempts in person, there are plenty of online courses you can explore to get started.

Join a Team

Being a part of a team can build trust for Gemini. He is always on the lookout for relationships that can grow and deepen over time. Team sports like softball provide Gemini with the opportunity to develop a comradery with his teammates based on a common goal: to win! Not only will joining a team sport offer Gemini a social outlet, but also it will spark his competitive side. Look for team sport leagues in your area that interest you. Many communities have recreational volleyball, dodgeball, kickball, and even soccer leagues that you can join during the appropriate weather season.

Embrace Your Twin Mind

When it comes to activities and outings, Gemini, you should likely plan to do two things at a time to fend off boredom and keep yourself entertained. This doubling up feeds your twin mind and keeps you interested. For example, if you go to the movies during the day, go to the ballet at night. If you spend the day playing or exercising outside, go to a museum exhibit or reading in the evening. Balance your activities and give yourself variety. Gemini loves to try new things and learn new information, so always be on the lookout for fun, new dual adventures you can try.

Learn Calligraphy

If you're an air sign, you're all about communication. Get creative with your communication style and study calligraphy! Calligraphy is a beautiful writing form that can take a lot of practice to master but can also be a rewarding skill. You may be able to share your abilities for things like wedding invitations, announcements, or memorials.

Calligraphy can also be a meditative practice, giving overthinking air signs a much-needed mental break. Allow yourself time to slow down and focus on each careful, deliberate movement instead of worrying about a problem at hand. Taking a break to focus on your calligraphy will help you redirect your attention and feel refreshed.

Join a Gym

———————

Joining a gym can be an intimidating feat, but Gemini needs a healthy channel to release his energy. Join a gym with a lot of options for you to try out. Doing the same physical exercise not only gets boring, but doesn't benefit your body as much as you'd think. After doing an exercise over and over, your body gets used to it. To keep your muscles challenged, always try to do something new.

A gym with classes is a great place to explore your options. You can try beginners' spinning, Zumba, yoga, Pilates, and so much more. Many gyms offer luxury services as well, such as a spa, swimming pool, sauna, and so on. Strike the perfect wellness balance by doing a challenging workout followed up by a nice dose of relaxation.

Take Up Tennis

Take some inspiration from fellow air sign Serena Williams, and try tennis (or racquetball)! Many air signs experience bursts of energy, which work well for a sport like tennis. It's no surprise that tennis or racquetball can be great workouts that develop muscles, improve hand-eye coordination, and strengthen heart health. But as an intellectual air sign, you might also find you enjoy the tactical nature of the game. Your critical-thinking skills might help you figure out the techniques, moves, and patterns you need to win the game. Clear your mind from other thoughts and focus on keeping your movements strong and fluid.

Visit Some Butterflies

Air signs can be spontaneous and would love to head out on an airy getaway. Try visiting a butterfly sanctuary! A butterfly sanctuary is an indoor living space or conservatory designed specifically for the breeding, development, and safe display of butterflies. They also offer lots of opportunities to learn about the butterflies and the ways we can conserve and protect them!

This visit can be a great opportunity to take care of yourself physically since you can spend plenty of time walking around the garden areas. This enjoyable activity can also have emotional benefits. Your positive mood is sure to carry through into your day well after you leave the sanctuary.

Feed the Birds

All birds are friends to air signs—they share your free-spirited nature! You may find it soothing and calming to watch birds fly about. Why not encourage them to come to your yard by setting up a bird feeder? Different birds will like different foods, so try putting out a seed mix, suet, or even the popular black oil sunflower seed that attracts many different kinds of birds. Make sure to place your feeder in a safe place away from predators and windows. You may even want to get expert advice on adopting (and properly caring for) a parakeet, mynah bird, or canary as a pet from a local animal shelter!

Multitask When You Can

Not everyone has the ability to multitask as easily as Gemini does. Because of his twin spirit, he has the power to do more than one thing at the same time without compromising the quality of either action. Use your twin spirit to your advantage and multitask whenever possible. This will actually help keep you focused rather than split your attention. You do best when your mind is constantly stimulated. You may find that you can often move seamlessly back and forth between different projects without missing a beat. Embrace your superpower, but always keep tabs on your stress level. If you find that you are becoming overwhelmed, scale back and focus on one task for a period of time.

Dine Out with Friends

I n many cultures dinner time is a social experience as much as a nutritional one. In fact, in some European countries dinner can last for hours with multiple courses. Embrace the celebratory nature of dinner and try a new restaurant with friends. Mix things up, try a new cuisine, and indulge in a food you've never tried before. Gemini loves being social, and there's no better way to keep the conversation between friends going than around a large table with delicious food and drink. Follow your curiosity and maybe you'll discover your next great culinary love.

Slow Down

Sometimes Gemini's energy can get the best of him, and he ends up blowing through social interactions and relationships rather than really participating and engaging. That's because Gemini is so used to multitasking and jumping from one thing to the next that he is always looking to the future.

Don't let your drive keep you from being present. Find a deeper meaning in your interactions. This may entail listening more to your friends, allotting more time for a social engagement so you can really enjoy yourself, or spending some time alone to re-center yourself.

Try Online Gaming

Combine your love of being social with your love for using your mind by joining an online gaming community. There are many different options that you can try, from multiplayer action games to card games and more. For Gemini, the speed of the game is often key. Look for fast-paced games that keep you stimulated. And if you aren't in the mood to engage with others socially, you can always look to Solitaire to keep your mind sharp. No matter what you play, your Gemini skills will help you win. After all, Gemini rules the mind, so he is a natural when it comes to strategy, and his social prowess will help him appreciate connecting with other people from all around the world.

Enjoy the Morning Crossword

Sometimes, doing something to keep your mind sharp is an important way to take care of yourself. Successfully completing a challenging task can help you feel stimulated and ready to take on the next project that comes your way. For air signs who love language and are often great problem-solvers, a crossword puzzle is a great way to exercise your mind. A word puzzle also has the added benefit of helping you learn new vocabulary, which air signs will love. Establish a new daily ritual and try doing your crossword puzzle in the morning—your success will help set the positive tone for the rest of the day!

Attend an Interesting Lecture

———

Air signs are naturally curious and love learning, so try attending a lecture or other form of presentation. Keep it fun and interesting by attending lectures on subjects that pique your curiosity. You may even be able to find presentations by popular speakers for free through your local library or other organizations in your area. Take some time for yourself to learn something new!

Doing something mentally stimulating will put all air signs in a good mood, but attending a lecture can also have an added social benefit. You may find yourself making friends with your fellow attendees as you discuss your shared interests after the event is over.

Go Orange

It's hard to get enough of the right nutrients in our diet in such a fast-paced world. With everything we need to accomplish in a day, we tend to just reach for the easiest and nearest food to keep our stomachs from growling. Try to be conscious of what you put into your body. Since Gemini rules over the lungs, start eating more orange fruits and vegetables. Foods like carrots, apricots, and pumpkins contain beta-carotene, which is thought to be helpful in maintaining lung health. Make these nutrient-dense foods a part of your daily diet and you'll start feeling stronger and healthier in no time.

Go Into Savasana

_____

Usually done at the end of a yoga practice, Savasana is a yoga pose that asks you to lie flat on your back with your arms a few inches from your side and your heels spread slightly apart. This pose is a wonderful way to rest and restore after a vigorous yoga class. Savasana is especially helpful for Gemini for two reasons: first, it helps ease tension in the shoulders and arms, and second, it allows Gemini time to focus on his thoughts and feelings. This pose can be a beneficial challenge to Gemini as you need to be fully awake yet fully relaxed at the same time.

Clear Your Mind
with Meditation

We've all heard about the many benefits of meditation: it can reduce stress, depression, and anxiety; increase happiness, focus, and self-awareness; and even improve your physical health. Some research has indicated that meditation can be helpful for everything from minor aches and pains and even the simple headache to major illnesses—including asthma, chronic pain, heart conditions, and cancer. Meditation is a perfect activity for air signs, who can use it to find balance and harmony in their everyday lives.

Use your meditation practice as an opportunity to stop overthinking and redirect your attention. Meditation will allow you to clear your mind and breathe, so you'll stay emotionally and physically healthy.

Think Through Your Decisions

A ir signs are great at critical thinking and like to make logical decisions. They'd rather follow their heads than let their emotions get in the way of their decision-making. Yet, because air signs like to take their time to see all sides of a question, making big decisions can prove difficult.

The best advice here is to not let yourself get rushed or pressured into making a decision. If you're feeling unbalanced, you can get trapped thinking in and out of hundreds of potential scenarios—many of which will never occur. If this happens, remember to take care of your emotions and your body; try doing some deep breathing and allowing your intuition to help you figure out which solutions are the best for you.

Moisturize Your Hands

While you may think that your face ages first, your hands are often the first area where you can see signs of aging. Gemini rules over the hands, so make it a priority to pamper your hands as often as possible. Start by buying a good-quality moisturizer and use it at least daily, or whenever your hands feel parched. You can also do deep moisturizing treatments at home for your hands, such as exfoliating the skin with a sugar scrub and rinsing, and then covering with a rich moisturizing lotion and moisturizing gloves overnight. When you wake up in the morning, your hands will be soft and silky.

Attend an Open Mic

There's nothing quite like the excitement and intimacy of live performance. Whether it's spoken word poetry, singing, or stand-up comedy, watching someone else bare their creative soul is an inspiring experience to behold. Attend a local open mic night at a local bar or restaurant to see firsthand the thrill of live performance. Gemini is a natural entertainer, but that doesn't mean that you have to be the one entertaining all the time. Just attending an open mic to support your fellow entertainers can be enough to temporarily satisfy your desire to perform. It will also give you new ideas to try out the next time you want to be center stage.

Celebrate Your Alone Time

———

Air signs are very social and are known for being great company because they can keep any situation from becoming too boring. However, it's important that you don't let yourself get burned out by spending all your time keeping other people entertained. It's good to take some time for yourself! Appreciate the time you have to spend doing something you like, whether that's heading outdoors or learning something new. Taking time to concentrate on yourself will give you a positive outlook and a fresh perspective. So instead of always focusing on others, reframe your mind-set and simply enjoy being alone.

Subscribe to New Podcasts

There are all kinds of ways to learn new information, and air signs are especially good at learning by listening. A great way for you to gather more information might be through podcasts. Podcasts are perfect for when you're on the go, since you can listen wherever you are, whether you're driving, grocery shopping, or even working out. There's a lot to learn, so choose a topic that you find interesting and simply search for the right podcast for you!

Listening to a podcast can also be a nice mental break. Centering your thoughts on whatever you're listening to can help you relax and redirect your mind away from any problem that's worrying you.

Create a Bright, Open Home

A ir signs are always on the move and can seem a little restless. So it's important that you use your home space as a place to restore and refocus. Create a beautiful, air-friendly home where you'll feel comfortable and able to relax.

Your design aesthetic is likely to be light, open, and airy. To start, don't set up your living spaces with so many components that they feel overcomplicated— simple spaces are important to air signs! Also, take some time to think about the lighting for your home. All the lights in your home should be full spectrum, which will help imitate the sunny outdoors, even on the rainiest days.

Decorate with Clear Quartz

Crystals can be a great way to add some beauty to a space and help rebalance your energy. Air signs will find lots of benefits from clear quartz crystals, which are among the most common and well-known healing stones. Learn about ways quartz may help treat you physically (crystal healing with clear quartz can be useful for the nervous system!) and mentally. Since clear quartz is believed to increase spiritual connections and clear thinking, it can be a useful tool when you need to expand your thoughts and think carefully.

Try decorating your home and office space with clear quartz crystal clusters so there's always one nearby when you start to feel a little off-balance.

Have a Good Laugh

Social air signs love to have a good time with their friends and family. Look for ways you can enjoy a laugh together! While the emotional and social benefits of sharing a laugh are clear, did you know laughter can also help your physical health by decreasing stress, lowering blood pressure, relieving pain, and even boosting your immune system? Taking some time to laugh every day will have a wide range of restorative benefits.

All you need to do is head to a comedy club or watch a silly movie. Or keep a book of puns, jokes, and limericks handy for when you need a pick-me-up or a reason to share a giggle with other people. Your love of language will make it doubly enjoyable for you!

Choose Light, Fresh Scents

A ir signs find it helpful for their living spaces to be well lit and spacious to mimic the natural world. So it makes sense that you'd also prefer lighter, more natural scents for your home. Whether you're looking for candles, room sprays, or other scented products, choose light scents like lemon verbena and rosewater. Even if you typically hate perfumes or colognes, these scents aren't overpowering. Instead, they'll make the air smell fresh and clean, which will help you feel more relaxed and at home in your living space. Certain scents also come with plenty of other benefits—for instance, a citrusy smell can help you feel a bit more energized!

Practice Color Meditation

Color meditation is a wonderful way to calm your mind and draw on the energies associated with different colors. Keep in mind that as a Gemini, to get the most out of your meditation, you should also add sound to your practice.

Focus on two colors when you practice color meditation: yellow and blue. Yellow speaks to the brightness of your soul and will help energize your spirit. Blue ties into the fact that you are an air sign and can symbolize the openness and freedom of the sky.

Whether it's a morning meditation to greet the day, or a restorative 15 minutes in the afternoon, find some time and a quiet place to meditate. Close your eyes, clear your mind, and focus on the two colors. Picture the bright yellow of the sun washing over your body. Feel it warm your skin and recharge your soul. Then envision the bluest of blue skies and allow that color to refresh your perspective, and imagine a life without boundaries.

Boost Your Immune System

Catching a cold is never a good thing—the coughing, the sneezing, the sore throat and fatigue. While no one is safe from the common cold, Gemini is particularly susceptible and can be quickly sidelined by its symptoms. As an act of self-care, be proactive during the cold season and protect yourself as best you can.

Strengthen your immune system with plenty of vitamin C, whether that means starting your day with a grapefruit, including orange slices as part of your afternoon snack, or brewing a pot of elderberry tea. Since Gemini rules the hands as well as the lungs, you'll also want to be mindful of your hands and the germs you may pick up during the height of cold season. So be sure to wash your hands often with soap and water. There's strength in knowing your weaknesses, and protecting against this one in particular will make your life much easier.

Find Balance Through Reiki

Sometimes an air sign can become unbalanced, perhaps due to overthinking or an issue with communication. When unbalanced, you may have difficulty being open-minded, and feel unwilling to accept new ideas—or you may feel overwhelmed with options. A Reiki treatment can be useful for reestablishing order in your life.

Reiki is a healing technique that aims to improve the movement of energy throughout the body through gentle touch. A Reiki session can cleanse your energy so it flows through your body smoothly and gets you back into balance. This practice will help you feel revitalized and refreshed, so be sure to consider setting up a session during high-stress times.

Try Feng Shui

It's important to get a good night's sleep so you wake up feeling enlivened and reinvigorated. For air signs, sleep is also an important aspect of keeping your nervous system in balance. Use the power of some basic feng shui to help you get exactly the right setup for better rest.

Feng shui is the practice of aligning and arranging elements in your home to create the ideal energy flow for positivity and good luck in various aspects of your life. To improve sleep, you should avoid positioning the bed so your feet point toward the bedroom door, which can decrease your personal energy. Considering things like the way other furniture in your bedroom can impede the flow of energy can also be helpful to improve your sleep.

Keep Your Hands Busy

In order to be productive, Gemini needs to stay focused. It's often hard to concentrate on a single task when your mind is going in a million different directions. One way to calm your mind and remain focused is by keeping your hands busy. Since Gemini rules the hands, it's best to keep them engaged while you're trying to concentrate. Play with a paper clip, keep some Silly Putty in a desk drawer, or doodle on your notepad. It may seem counterproductive, but by giving your hands something to do while you're working, you'll find it easier to stay on task. Your increased productivity will give you more time to do the things you actually enjoy!

Perform Random Acts
of Kindness

A ir signs can be extremely thoughtful; they're great at being objective when they need to be and genuinely want to see positive changes in the world around them. An easy way for air signs to help make a small change every day is to complete a random act of kindness. This can be anything from adding some extra coins to a parking meter that's about to run out to volunteering for a good cause. You could also pay for your coworker's coffee when you see them in the drive-thru line behind you, pack your partner's lunch for the day, or call an elderly relative just to chat about their week.

Making simple acts of kindness a daily ritual can strengthen your relationships by showing others how much you care about them, and can improve your own everyday outlook!

Enjoy a Rainy Day

Air signs are connected to the weather—after all, your mood can change just as quickly and drastically as the winds! Take some time to connect with and appreciate changes in the weather instead of letting them get you down. Don't let yourself get upset by a rainy day. Instead, enjoy a good rainstorm! Sit by your window and simply savor the wind and rain. You may find it helps you relax to bring a cup of tea with you or take a few deep, meditative breaths. By training yourself to look at things in a positive light, you'll take better care of your emotional needs and feel happier every day.

Balance Your Mind and Body
with Pilates

E ven though air signs are often focused on the mind, it's just as important to take care of the body through exercise. The secret to consistent exercise? Find a workout routine that works for you and that you enjoy! Not only will your body feel healthy and strong, but you'll also head into your workout with a much more positive attitude.

One routine that might work well for air signs is a Pilates class, which focuses on both the mind and the body as you work your way through different moves. You'll learn to strengthen your physique through careful movement, develop your flexibility and balance, and properly manage your breathing for less stress and more control of your body.

Put Eucalyptus in Your Shower

A nice, hot shower can be therapeutic on its own. With the warm water relaxing your muscles and refreshing your skin, a shower is the perfect way to start your day or a great idea if you are looking to unwind after a stressful one. What can make it even better for you, Gemini, is hanging a bundle of eucalyptus behind your shower head.

The steam activates the plant's natural healing properties, which work wonders on your respiratory system. Tie a few branches together with some string or twine, and then let the bundle hang against the shower wall (out of the direct water stream). The heat from the water will release the eucalyptus oils into the air, turning your already relaxing hot shower into a full aromatic experience with revitalizing steam.

Invest in an Air Purifier

As an air sign, you know that the quality of the air around you is important for your health and well-being. Clean air is especially important for your physical health if you have asthma or other lung issues, but the truth is that everyone can benefit! Keeping dust, smog, and other tiny particles out of your lungs is an important way to not only keep you feeling your best, but also helps prevent other illnesses. Research and invest in a good air purifier to help eliminate things like pollen, smoke, or other pollutants from the air in your home. An air purifier can be especially important if you live in a city where the increased population and traffic can mean more pollution.

Keep Healthy Snacks at Hand

As a Gemini you're always on the go, which means you need to refuel your body often. It's important to be mindful of what you're eating though. Since you're constantly going, going, going, it's easy to choose foods for their convenience rather than their nourishing properties. But, by taking the time to prepare some snacks, you'll be able to use those eating opportunities as a chance to strengthen your mind and body.

Find a healthy trail mix recipe that includes your favorites, or use your creativity to come up with your own combination. The mix of sweet and savory speaks to the duality of your sign and offers the chance to enjoy a mix of nuts, seeds, dried fruit, and dark chocolate that is packed with vitamins and nutrients. Plus, snacking on trail mix helps to keep those Gemini fingers busy!

Upgrade Your Technology

Can you even imagine a time before cell phones, Gemini? Technology has come on in leaps and bounds over the past few years, and, luckily, you are a forward thinker who is always ready to embrace the next wave of technological advancement.

If you haven't already, you should now upgrade your technology, Gemini, especially if you haven't experienced the wonder and innovation of voice-activated devices. Typing is so yesterday. Now all it takes is a simple voice command followed by a question and your device will do the work for you. This is very helpful for Gemini since you are always multitasking, looking for a way to streamline how you live and work. You are also a fantastic communicator, so using your voice will feel natural compared to typing on tiny screens.

Cleanse Your Home by Smudging

The state of your mind is often reflected in the state of your home. If there's clutter everywhere and dust is starting to gather, there's a good chance you're feeling stuck emotionally and mentally as well. For intellectual air signs, this clutter can make you feel unbalanced and distressed. Smudging is a simple cleansing ritual that you can use to clear out negativity in your home (and also your mind!) and inspire a fresh, positive start.

All you'll need to get started is some ceremonial sage (not the type found in the spice aisle at grocery stores) or palo santo sticks, a fireproof bowl, and some matches or a lighter. Tidy up any obvious clutter and open as many doors and windows as possible in your home. Place the sage or palo santo in a fire-proof bowl and light the stick. Blow it out and use the fireproof bowl to hold the smoking stick as you walk around your home, spreading the smoke throughout and focusing on its ability to remove negativity. Make way for a refreshed, positive attitude!

Learn to Dance

Fluid, airy movements are aesthetically pleasing to air signs, so you may enjoy watching ballet or modern dance. If you're feeling ready to jump up and start dancing yourself, consider signing up for a class to learn more about those styles. Dance has a lot of benefits for your physical health—you can develop your strength, increase your flexibility, and improve your posture. But it can also be an effective way to relieve stress and build confidence. As you focus on learning specific steps and developing your skills, you'll have the opportunity to clear your mind so you feel refreshed and ready to take on the rest of the day.

Catch Up with Friends

Your propensity for being a social butterfly often makes you the life of the party, but it can also keep you from connecting with people on a deeper level. Take time to check in with your close friends by inviting them out for a one-on-one catch-up date. This may mean meeting up at a local coffee spot to chat, or it may mean inviting them to your place for a cocktail and appetizers. Make sure to keep it low key and focused. Your goal is to really connect with someone who means a lot to you, without a lot of distraction. Not only will your soul thank you later, but your friends will feel especially loved and cared for.

Research a New Health Trend

Get your brain involved in your self-care, Gemini. Start by researching the hottest new health trends to see if there is something you'd like to try. Look for current studies and statistics about how well it works and if there are any concerns about its impact on well-being. If you read that a food, vitamin, or immune-enhancing practice is good for your mind, body, or spirit, you are more likely to add it to your self-care routine. There's nothing wrong with needing evidence that something will help before you make it a habit. Next, check with your doctor for their advice. Do your diligence and see what you can find!

De-Stress with Kiteflying

S ometimes, acting like a kid is a great way to release stress. And what is a better throwback activity for an air sign than flying a kite! Air signs can easily get wrapped up in their own thoughts, so an activity like flying kites that gets you out into the natural world, and gives you something to take your mind off your worries, can be a big help for your stress level. If you find you really enjoy kiteflying, you might consider checking out a kiteflying competition to develop your skills even more, and make some new friends. You may even get a little exercise from chasing your kite around!

Go on a Weekly Hike

A ir signs need to spend plenty of time out in the fresh air, so they're likely to feel reenergized after heading out for a hike. If you go out to the woods or fields, you'll get a chance to view some beautiful scenery while you walk.

You can also combine your appreciation for the outdoors with your workout schedule! Hiking is a great workout that can improve heart health, strengthen muscles, and increase stability and balance. It's also often recommended as a natural stress-relief activity. It's just as important to take care of your body as it is your mind, so add a weekly hike to your workouts!

Try Qigong

Q igong is a form of gentle exercise where participants do a series of repetitive motions, stretching the body and increasing fluid movement in the joints and muscles. It is also a form of meditation that can promote stress relief through controlled breathing and spatial awareness. It is an ancient Chinese tradition that has been used for thousands of years to help prevent chronic pain, ease depression and anxiety, and build muscle strength. Try a beginners' class and incorporate this tranquil practice into your self-care routine, Gemini. Its soothing nature will help quiet your mind and give you a chance to zen out, while your body will adapt to each movement and release tension at the same time.

Find an Online Community

As a Gemini you have a lot of thoughts and interests, so why not share them? Thanks to social media, we live in a highly connected world. People from across the globe can converse daily as if they were sitting right next to one another. Use this technology to your advantage, Gemini. Find a subreddit on *Reddit*, a *Facebook* group, or some other positive online community that shares your interests and passions. Engage in conversation with its members, and see what you can learn from them. You never know what kind of connections you can make until you try!

Learn about the Weather

Air signs are sensitive to changes in the weather, so you're already likely to be very aware of the changes in the air around you. You can encourage your intellectual interests and take better care of your physical self by learning a little more about the weather. Purchase an old-fashioned barometer to keep in your home.

A barometer is a scientific instrument that's often used to predict the weather because it measures changes in the atmospheric pressure. High pressure usually indicates good weather, but watch out if that level starts to drop! Not only will you learn a fun new piece of information to share, you'll also be prepared no matter the weather with just a glance at your barometer.

Release Sky Lanterns

Create time for yourself to take care of your spiritual needs! If you've recently experienced a loss of someone from your life, it is important to honor both those people and your own feelings. Turn to your air sign–inspired appreciation for nature and call upon the energy in the air around you for some help by releasing a fire-retardant sky lantern. (Just be sure to check regulations in your area and research the safest method and locations for releasing the lanterns before doing so.) Simply write a message on the lantern to your loved one and then release it into the sky. Allowing the air, your influencing element, to carry your message where it needs to be can give you the closure and release you've been seeking.

Hang Some Mirrors

Gemini has dual sides working together to make up a whole, hence the zodiac symbol of Twins. To tap into your own duality, try hanging double mirrors around your home so you can see yourself from multiple angles. This may help you discover different parts of yourself and who you really are. But be careful! Whatever you do, do not hang two mirrors in your bedroom. It is bad for feng shui and may disrupt positive energy flow. You only want good energy where you begin and end your day.

Try Chewing Gum

Chewing gum is a good relaxant for Gemini, and can often help him think. In fact, some studies have even found that chewing gum can improve concentration and boost memory while combating stress and anxiety, all positives for a weary Gemini. But be aware, not all gum is created equal. When choosing one to chomp on, look for gum that is all-natural and free of chemicals that can hurt your teeth. Also be careful to give your jaw a rest if you find that your chewing is causing muscle tension.

Listen to Conversation Around You

Air signs are the element of communication, so it's only natural for you to pay attention to the conversations around you. You're also always ready to learn new things, so you're likely to be listening for subjects that might pique your interest. Whether you're riding the subway, waiting in line at the super-market, or mingling at a party, you're sure to catch some snippets of chatter that grab your attention. You might even consider carrying around a notebook and pen to jot down little bits of conversation you hear or interesting topics you'd like to learn more about later.

Take Care of Yourself

I f you're an air sign, you know you can sometimes get trapped in your own head. Air signs are intellectual people, which makes them great problem-solvers and critical thinkers. However, there's always the risk of overthinking and spending too much time living in your mind. Don't let yourself get too detached from daily life!

Completing necessary, practical activities is essential self-care. Things like eating three good meals a day, showering, and brushing your teeth every morning and evening are important for keeping your life in balance. So remember to stay grounded in the real world and do the things you need to do to keep yourself healthy and happy.

About the Author

Constance Stellas is an astrologer of Greek heritage with more than twenty-five years of experience. She primarily practices in New York City and counsels a variety of clients, including business CEOs, artists, and scholars. She has been interviewed by *The New York Times*, *Marie Claire*, and *Working Woman*, and has appeared on several New York TV morning shows, featuring regularly on Sirius XM and other national radio programs as well. Constance is the astrologer for *HuffPost* and a regular contributor to Thrive Global. She is also the author of several titles, including *The Astrology Gift Guide*, *Advanced Astrology for Life*, *The Everything® Sex Signs Book*, and the graphic novel series Tree of Keys, as well as coauthor of *The Hidden Power of Everyday Things*. Learn more about Constance at her website, ConstanceStellas.com, or on *Twitter* (@Stellastarguide).